CHICKENS DON'T FLY

and other fun facts

For my friend Tilly
—L. D.

For Joe
—H. E.

For Brittany and Oliver
—P. O.

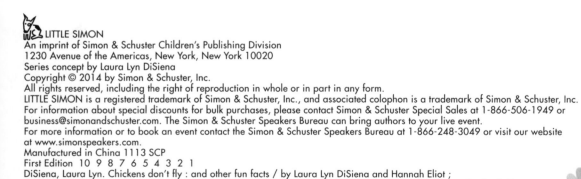

LITTLE SIMON
An imprint of Simon & Schuster Children's Publishing Division
1230 Avenue of the Americas, New York, New York 10020
Series concept by Laura Lyn DiSiena
Copyright © 2014 by Simon & Schuster, Inc.
For information about special discounts for bulk purchases, please contact Simon & Schuster Special Sales at 1-866-506-1949 or
business@simonandschuster.com. The Simon & Schuster Speakers Bureau can bring authors to your live event.
For more information or to book an event contact the Simon & Schuster Speakers Bureau at 1-866-248-3049 or visit our website
at www.simonspeakers.com.
Manufactured in China 1113 SCP
First Edition 10 9 8 7 6 5 4 3 2 1
DiSiena, Laura Lyn. Chickens don't fly : and other fun facts / by Laura Lyn DiSiena and Hannah Eliot ;
illustrated by Pete Oswald. — 1st ed. p. cm. — (Did you know?) Summary: "A book of fun facts about animals of all sizes,
shapes, and species!"— Provided by publisher. Audience: 4-8. Audience: K to grade 3. Includes bibliographical references
and index. ISBN 978-1-4424-9326-1 (pbk : alk. paper) — ISBN 978-1-4424-9353-7 (hc : alk. paper) —
ISBN 978-1-4424-9327-8 (ebook) 1. Chickens—Miscellanea—Juvenile literature. 2. Animals—Miscellanea—Juvenile literature.
3. Children's questions and answers. I. Eliot, Hannah. II. Oswald, Pete, ill. III. Title. IV. Title: Chickens do not fly.
SF487.5.D57 2014 590.2—dc23 2013009392

DID YOU KNOW?

CHICKENS DON'T FLY

and other fun facts

By Laura Lyn DiSiena and Hannah Eliot
Illustrated by Pete Oswald

LITTLE SIMON
New York   London   Toronto   Sydney   New Delhi

WELL, HELLO!

Did you know that female chickens are called hens and male chickens are called roosters?

Or that female chickens lay about 1 egg each day?

Hello MY NAME IS Hen

Hello MY NAME IS Rooster

JULY

How about that there are more chickens in the world than any other kind of bird?

OKAY, MAYBE YOU KNEW THOSE THINGS.

But did you know that chickens don't **FLY**?
Chickens aren't *completely* flightless, though.
They can flutter into the air high enough to
make it over a fence or into a tree.

But that's nothing compared to what the peregrine falcon can do. When the falcon is hunting, it soars high into the sky and then makes a steep dive to catch its prey—sometimes at more than 200 miles per hour! That makes the peregrine falcon not only the fastest bird, but the fastest ANIMAL on the planet!

SHOW OFF.

With their long claws and superstrong grip, sloths are built for living in trees. Most sloths spend about half their day hanging from branches—and the other half sleeping in those branches!

Salamanders are amphibians,
so they spend part of their life on
land and part in water.

When on land, some salamanders can make their feet suction to surfaces—like trees—so they can climb upside down!

HELLo.

Spotted salamanders are nocturnal. This means they are only active at night! During the day, they rest and hide under rocks, logs and leaves. Sometimes they even take cover in burrows made by other animals!

Did you know that most sharks need to keep swimming in order to to breathe? When they swim, they take in water through their gills and turn it into oxygen.

But scientists discovered a place in Mexico called the Cave of Sleeping Sharks, where there's enough oxygen that sharks can breathe without moving. Phew! They get to take a rest!

The largest fish is the whale shark—it can grow to be more than 40-feet long. But sharks can be really small, too. Some, like the dwarf lantern shark, are only about 8 inches!

A thorny devil is a lizard that lives in central Australia. It also grows to be 8-inches long. You would think that something this small would be an easy target for larger animals, but as its name suggests, this lizard is covered with sharp thorns to scare off predators.

WATCH OUT!

The speediest land animal of them all is the cheetah. When *its* predators come along, the cheetah does what it's best at and RUNS! Can you count to 1...2...?

This big cat can accelerate to 45 miles per hour in the time it took you to count those two seconds. That takes a lot of energy!

A cheetah has a long tail, but the land mammal with the absolute longest tail is the giraffe. A giraffe's tail can be up to 8-feet long! They also have super-long necks, so it's not very surprising that giraffes are the tallest animals on earth. They are about 14-feet to 19-feet tall!

Polar bears may not be the world's tallest animal, but did you know that they are the world's largest bear? Polar bears mostly live in the Arctic Circle, and have large, flattened feet with webbing between their toes. This webbing helps them swim, and the rough pads on their paws help them walk on slippery ice!

The polar bear's white coat camouflages it in the surrounding snow and ice. But under their fur, polar bears actually have dark skin. This keeps them warm by soaking up the sun's rays. A polar bear's only visible skin is on it's nose.

WHERE'D HE GO?

Speaking of noses, elephants are some of the largest land mammals around, and they sure do have BIG noses! But an elephant's trunk is a lot more than just a nose: it makes noises and grabs things, like food.

SNiFF
SNiFF
SNiFF

Elephants also have an extremely good sense of smell. They can detect a water source that's 12 miles away!

The bloodhound is another animal with a great sense of smell. It is so good at scent-tracking, in fact, that bloodhounds are often used to find criminal evidence.

And that evidence can be used in the courtroom!

Did you hear that? It sounds like someone is laughing . . . oh, it's a hyena! That's the sound hyenas make when they want to let one another know they've found food. Hyenas live in clans with as many as 80 members. Staying in groups is a way for them to protect themselves from predators on the African plains—such as lions!

Have you ever heard of a platypus? It's kind of a funny-looking animal. The platypus has a curved bill like a duck, a wide, flat tail like a beaver, and webbed feet like a frog! It's so unique, in fact, that when scientists first discovered it in 1798, they didn't believe it was real. They thought someone was playing a prank on them!

Like hyenas, platypuses have predators. And like hyenas, platypuses *are* predators. Platypuses have a very special ability called electroreception. This means that when they dive in to the water, they find their prey partly by sensing electric fields—the electricity helps them figure out where the animals are! Because platypuses have this sense, they actually close their eyes and ears when they go underwater for food!

Bees have eyes but they don't have ears! Bees live in colonies, and in each colony, there is a queen bee. A queen bee uses her stinger to lay eggs—up to 2,000 each day!

Wow, that's more eggs than some chickens will lay in a lifetime. And unlike chickens, bees sure do fly!

MORE FUN FACTS

Bloodhound: The bloodhound dog breed is more than 1,000 years old!

Shark: Some sharks lose 30,000 or more teeth in their lifetime. Most humans usually only lose 20!

Polar bear: When they are born, polar bear babies are the size of a rat and weigh a little more than a pound!

Platypus: The platypus has also been called water mole, duckbill, and duckmole.

Sloth: Although they are slow in trees, three-toed sloths are quick swimmers.

Chicken: Chickens are probably the closest living relatives of the Tyrannosaurus rex.

Bee: Bees see all colors except the color red. Flowers that attract bees are usually yellow, blue, or purple.

Salamander: If a salamander loses its tail, it can make the tail grow back!

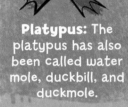

Giraffe: A giraffe's tongue is black!

Elephant: Elephants use their tusks to dig for food and water, and strip bark from trees.

Cheetah: Female cheetahs are solitary and usually live alone, whereas male cheetahs tend to live in groups.

Peregrine falcon: Peregrine falcons make their nests in lots of different environments—including bridges and skyscrapers!

Hyena: When a hyena's tail sticks straight up, usually the hyena is about to attack. When a hyena tucks its tail between its legs, the hyena is frightened.

Thorny devil: A thorny devil can camouflage itself by changing colors.